Dear Parent:

Remember the first time you read a book by yourself? I do. I still remember the thrill of reading the words Little Bear said to Mother Bear: "I have a new space helmet. I am going to the moon."

Later when my daughter was learning to read, her favorite I Can Read books were the funny ones—Danny playing with the dinosaur he met at the museum and Amelia Bedelia dressing the chicken. And now as a new teacher, she has joined the thousands of teachers who use I Can Read books in the classroom.

I'm delighted to share this commemorative edition with you. This special volume includes the origin stories and early sketches of many beloved I Can Read characters.

Here's to the next sixty years—and to all those beginning readers who are about to embark on a lifetime of discovery that starts with the magical words *"I can read!"*

Kate M. Jackson
Senior VP, Associate Publisher, Editor-in-Chief

Pinkalicious®

Tutu-rrific

For Lilly
—V.K.

The author gratefully acknowledges the artistic and
editorial contributions of Daniel Griffo and Natalie Engel.

I Can Read Book® is a trademark of HarperCollins Publishers.

Pinkalicious: Tutu-rrific
Copyright © 2014 by Victoria Kann

PINKALICIOUS and all related logos and characters are trademarks of Victoria Kann. Used with permission.

Based on the HarperCollins book *Pinkalicious* written by
Victoria Kann and Elizabeth Kann, illustrated by Victoria Kann.
All rights reserved.

www.icanread.com

Library of Congress Control Number: 2014935753
ISBN 978-0-06-257278-3

18   19   20   21   WOZ   10 9 8 7 6 5 4 3 2   ❖   First Edition

Pinkalicious®
Tutu-rrific

by Victoria Kann

HARPER

An Imprint of HarperCollinsPublishers

Alison and I giggled as we tried
to balance on our toes.
Tomorrow we were going
to ballet class together!
I was pink with glee.

I had never taken

a ballet class before,

but Alison had.

"You'll love it," she said.

"We twirl and jump through the air

and spin on our tippy-toes."

"What fun!" I said.

"What's your outfit like?" I asked.

"It's a purple tutu,"

said Alison.

"What does yours look like?"

I laughed and said, "Guess!"

The next day, I got ready:

I wore my pink tutu,

pink slippers,

and pink bows in my hair.

Mommy took me to class.

When we got there, I thought I saw

a purple tutu.

"There's Alison!" I said.

I ran inside to catch Alison.

There were people all over!

I thought I saw a flash of purple

run into a room.

"Alison, wait!" I called.

But Alison didn't hear me.

I followed her into the class.

I couldn't spot her

with all the dancers.

Just then, the teacher walked in.

"Okay, everyone!" she said.

"Take your place at the barre."

I'd have to find Alison later.

"Time to warm up," said the teacher.

"First position," she called.

I looked around the room.

Everyone was moving their feet.

Heels together, toes apart.

This was easy!

"Plié," the teacher sang.

The ballerinas bent their knees,

so I did, too.

Piece of cake!

"Very good," said the teacher.

"Now, let's go over

the dance we learned last week."

I didn't know the moves,

but I wasn't worried.

Ballet seemed really, really simple.

The teacher put on some music.

The dancers moved their arms,

first up, then down.

Then they kicked their legs

up and down.

I followed along just fine.

Suddenly, the music got faster.

The girls skipped in a circle

and jumped in the air.

I was stuck in the middle,

not sure what to do.

Everyone moved so quickly.

I couldn't keep up!

When I hopped, they kicked.

When I kicked, they swayed.

"Hold on!" I cried.

But no one could hear me!

I looked around for Alison,

but she wasn't there.

It was a girl who looked like Alison.

I had made a mistake.

I knew I had to say something.

I stopped dancing and raised my hand.

"Excuse me," I said.

"I think I'm in the wrong class!"

Just as I put my hand up,

the dancers jumped up high.

"Beautiful!" said the teacher.

She didn't see me!

I tried to get out of the circle,

but the dancers linked arms.

I tried crawling through their legs,

but the dancers hopped up and down.

"Wait!" I shouted,

but nothing helped.

I was trapped between tutus

with no way out.

"Get ready for the grand finale!"
the teacher called out.

I gulped.

The girls spread out their arms
and started twirling.

"Oh!" I said, happily surprised.

They were spinning!

I could do this!

I took a deep breath

and twirled and whirled

and spun around.

I was spinning so freely,
I didn't notice that everyone
had stopped.

The teacher looked at me, confused.

"You!" she said.

"You're not in this class!"

"Uh-oh," I whispered.

I was sure I was in trouble.

Instead, the teacher just smiled.

"You must be in the wrong room," she said.

"I'll have someone walk you to the beginner class.

But first, could you spin again?"

I twirled around once more.

"You're so graceful!" said the teacher.

"Keep practicing and soon
you will be in my advanced class."

In the beginner class,

I told Alison what happened.

"What was it like?" she asked.

"It was tutu-rrific!" I said,

and did a pirouette.

"I can read! I can read!
Where are the books for me?"

One question from a young reader sparked a reading revolution!

A conversation between the director of Harper's Department of Books for Boys and Girls, Ursula Nordstrom, and Boston Public Library's Virginia Haviland inspired the I Can Read book series. Haviland told Nordstrom that a young boy had burst into the children's reading room and asked her where he could find books that were just right for a brand-new reader like himself.

Determined to fill this gap, Nordstrom published *Little Bear* by Else Holmelund Minarik, with illustrations by Maurice Sendak, in the fall of 1957. The response was immediate. According to the *New York Times*, "One look at the illustrations and children will grab for it. A second look at the short, easy sentences, the repetition of words, and the beautiful type spacing, and children will know they can read it themselves."

Delightful and wonderfully warm, *Little Bear* served as the template for the series, and now, sixty years later, we have over four hundred I Can Read stories for our youngest and newest readers!

Where the Ideas for the Characters Came From

Berenstain Bears

Stan and Jan Berenstain were cartoonists in the 1950s. When their sons began to read, they submitted a story about a family of bears to author, editor, and publisher Ted Geisel (aka Dr. Seuss), which was published as *The Big Honey Hunt* in 1962. Geisel labeled their next effort "Another Adventure of the Berenstain Bears." That's how the bears got their name!

Biscuit

One day while watching her daughter play with their neighbor's frisky dog, Alyssa Capucilli was struck by her daughter's patience and gentle nature, as well as the fact that her little girl thought the dog understood every word she said. That was the inspiration for the little yellow puppy and his sweet companion. Pat Schories's warm illustrations capture their tender relationship.

Pete the Cat

When James Dean first saw Pete, he was a tiny black kitten in a shelter. Pete looked like he had been starved and his black fur was a mess. At first, James had no interest in Pete—black cats were bad luck, after all! But the scrawny little fellow stuck his paw out of the cage, wanting to play! James took Pete home. And even though James chose to paint Pete the Cat blue (his favorite color), James realizes now that black cats are actually very good luck.

Danny and the Dinosaur

In 1958, cartoonist Syd Hoff's daughter Susan was going through a rough surgery, and one day, Syd decided to draw a picture to cheer her up. It showed a dinosaur with Syd's brother on its back. When Susie saw the picture, she exclaimed, "Danny and the dinosaur!" and that night after the family went to bed, Syd wrote the story.

Pinkalicious

Victoria Kann's daughters could never seem to get enough of cupcakes or the color pink! One year, as an April Fools' joke, Victoria told her family and friends that one of her daughters had turned pink from eating too many pink cupcakes—and so the idea for *Pinkalicious* was born!

Frog and Toad

The characters of Frog and his best friend, Toad, might have been inspired by . . . a horror movie! Arnold Lobel and his daughter, Adrianne, went to see a movie called *Frogs* at the drive-in. However, the movie featured not frogs, but toads! Adrianne told her dad about the many differences between the two—and two years later the first Frog and Toad book, *Frog and Toad Are Friends*, appeared.

Little Critter

Mercer Mayer was doodling around one day in 1974 when he drew a shape like a gourd, put two eyes on it, scribbled a nose connecting the eyes, then got coffee and forgot about it! The next day, he noticed a small piece of paper on the floor. It was his gourd. He added fuzzy hair and a big mouth; short stubby arms and feet. Mercer had created a fuzzy little "woodchuck-y porcupine" thing that became Little Critter!

Fancy Nancy

When Jane O'Connor was a small girl, every Sunday, when her grandma and great aunts came to visit, Jane would greet them at the door in a tutu and a pair of her mom's high heels. She thought she looked très glamorous!

Years later, while she was fixing dinner one night, the name Fancy Nancy flew into Jane's head, and a star made her debut!

Amelia Bedelia

Amelia Bedelia was inspired by Peggy Parish's third-grade students at the Dalton School in New York City. The children mixed up words, and Parish found them hilarious. That gave Parish the idea for Amelia Bedelia—a character who takes every word literally and embraces life with an outlook that is forthright and optimistic. Illustrator Fritz Siebel worked with Parish to create the perfect look for the conscientious cleaning lady.

Early Character Development

The Berenstain Bears

Stan and Jan Berenstain's early sketches from *The Berenstain Bears Clean House*

Pete the Cat

James Dean's first painting of Pete the Cat

Frog and Toad

Early character sketch of Frog and Toad

Biscuit

Biscuit character sketches

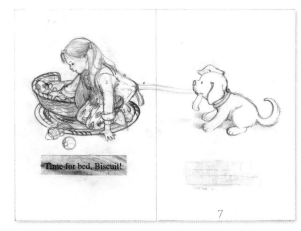

Pat Schories's early sketches from *Biscuit*

Pinkalicious

Victoria Kann's sketches for the picture book *Pinkalicious*

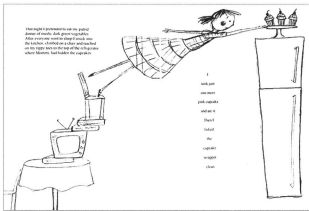

Amelia Bedelia

Fritz Siebel's sketches for the picture book *Amelia Bedelia*

Danny and the Dinosaur

Syd Hoff's early cover sketches for *Danny and the Dinosaur*

Little Critter

Mercer Mayer's early character sketches of Little Critter

Fancy Nancy

Robin Preiss Glasser's character sketches and cover sketch for *Fancy Nancy and the Boy from Paris*

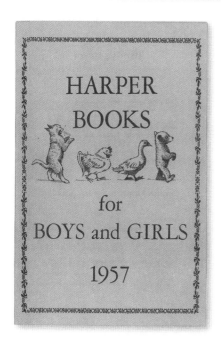

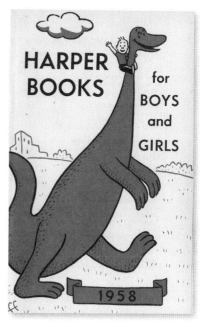

These two catalogs marked the launch of I Can Read!

Sixty Years of I CAN READ

1957 Little Bear

 1958 Danny and the Dinosaur

1959 Sammy the Seal

Emmett's Pig

1960 Cat and Dog

1961 Little Bear's Visit*

 1963 Amelia Bedelia

1970 Frog and Toad Are Friends*

A Bargain for Frances

1972 Frog and Toad Together**

1984 In a Dark, Dark Room and Other Scary Stories

1986 The Josefina Story Quilt

1996 Biscuit

2005 The Berenstain Bears Clean House

2008 Fancy Nancy and the Boy from Paris

Little Critter: Snowball Soup

2010 Pinkalicious: School Rules!

2013 Pete the Cat: Pete's Big Lunch

2017 Long, Tall Lincoln

* Caldecott Honor titles
** Newbery Honor